D0912202

Somewhere to Follow

Somewhere to Follow

~*Poems*~

PAUL J. WILLIS

SOMEWHERE TO FOLLOW
Poems

Copyright © 2021 Paul J. Willis. All rights reserved. Except for brief quotations in critical publications or reviews, no part of this book may be reproduced in any manner without prior written permission from the publisher. Write: Permissions, Wipf and Stock Publishers, 199 W. 8th Ave., Suite 3, Eugene, OR 97401.

Slant
An Imprint of Wipf and Stock Publishers
199 W. 8th Ave., Suite 3
Eugene, OR 97401

www.wipfandstock.com

HARDCOVER ISBN: 978-1-7252-5696-5
PAPERBACK ISBN: 978-1-7252-5695-8
EBOOK ISBN: 978-1-7252-5697-2

Cataloguing-in-Publication data:

Names: Willis, Paul J.

Title: Somewhere to follow: poems. / Paul J. Willis.

Description: Eugene, OR: Slant, 2021.

Identifiers: ISBN 978-1-7252-5696-5 (hardcover) | ISBN 978-1-7252-5695-8 (paperback) | ISBN 978-1-7252-5697-2 (ebook)

Subjects: LCSH: American poetry — 21st century. | Nature — Poetry. | Trees — Poetry. | Flowers — Poetry.

Classification: PS3573.I456555 S66 2021 (paperback) | PS3573.I456555 S66 (ebook)

06/02/21

For

Micah and J-Bear,

on your way . . .

Contents

III. Near

IV. Far

SOMEWHERE TO FOLLOW

No one knows where this trail goes.
No sign at the trailhead lists the miles,
the destinations. No map is marked
with a dotted line. And yet the path
appears at your feet, disappears
between two trees, an invisible door.

Once you set out this slender way,
do not look back, for the trail
will have vanished behind you.
No one else can come this far:
this path is a lamp for your feet only.

I.

Then

CAMPFIRE PROGRAM

There in front of the fire circle, in your big-brimmed ranger hat,
you stand at ease, arms waving hundreds of voices into song
under the flashing redwood trees. *On Top of Old Smokey,*

O My Darling, She'll Be Comin' Round the Mountain.
And the singers, in their plaid flannel shirts, their pedal-pushers,
roasted marshmallows still sticky upon their fingers,

all swell in time and in tune as your palm now makes
invisible triangles in air, lofting the measures to the stars.
This is America in the Fifties, relieved to be quit of the good war,

and proud to have won it, and glad to have issued
from their roomy canvas tents parked next to their automobiles.
And look there, Ranger, your young wife from the orange grove

is sitting on the split-log bench in the front row, your two-year-old
pulling on her sleeve—your young wife who is tired and queasy
and four months pregnant with me, and about to come down with polio,

though she does not know it and neither do you. She is gazing
at you with admiration, and you think, yes, O my darling,
one more verse, folks, and just the women this time.

—*Big Basin Redwoods State Park*

CRIME AND PUNISHMENT

I am six years old. My brother and I are trampolining
on my bed on a summer morning, and I end up on a dismount
between the mattress and the wall, chin on the covers.

My brother senses an opening—or a closing, rather—
and shoves the bed against the wall, trapping me tight.
"Help!" I call, hoping Mom is in earshot. "*Help! Help!*"

He shoves harder, and there goes the air from my lungs.
"*Hel*—!" I say, not making it to the final *p*. Mom comes
limping into the room, hands red and wet from washing the dishes.

"Mom!" he cries, his face contorted in pious horror.
"He said *Hell!*" Mom plucks me from behind the bed,
not even noticing, which is unlike her, that I am half-asphyxiated.

She holds me firmly at arm's length, tells me what I already know.
"But—but," I say. "No *buts*," she orders. "Your father will deal
with this when he gets home." Over her shoulder, my brother grins.

That afternoon, Dad takes me solemnly into the backyard.
Asks me to drop my drawers. Tells me that this hurts him
more than it hurts me. But when his hand comes smacking

down across my rear, I can only think through my hot tears,
through the wet snot bubbling out of my nose,
that that just can't be true. Hell, it could never be true.

IN FEAR OF ART

When Mrs. Albright visited
our classroom in her busy smock,
I cowered while the others cheered.
How could one line possibly
lead into another?

And why smear charcoal
where we might form letters
of the alphabet, the beautiful letters
pulling in a heavenly train
on parallel tracks above the board?

For this I knew, as well
as I knew that Jesus loved me:
Thou shalt make no graven image.
But *write thee all the words*
I have spoken upon the scroll.

So I sat there, quiet, staring
at my empty paper, watercolors
ready at hand. And all around me,
classmates freshening their dreams,
calling like sparrows across the room.

Mrs. Albright, why are you
still grabbing the paintbrush
out of my fingers, making it dart
like a thin blue lizard
across the desert of my page?

WHAT BOYS DO

Dig a hole in the empty lot out back.
Not for treasure, though they find
an ancient Coke bottle or two,

some earth-rich worms. When the hole
gets deep enough, roof it with a scrap
of plywood, shovel dirt over the top.

Then wriggle down through an open
corner, crowd into that nest of clay,
carve a niche for a stolen candle.

No other purpose, just a place to listen
to each other's breathing, tell stories
of other boys, buried alive, underground.

BY GRACE ARE YE SAVED

It's a Saturday. I am practicing scales on the piano
when the doorbell rings—and I'm glad
to have a reason to stop. A huddle of strangers,
all in black, looms through the panel of wavy glass.

"Mom?" I call. She limps from the kitchen,
opens the door, stands firm. "Good morning,"
they say, chorus-like, men and women—skirts, ties.
"Are you sure of your salvation when the end cometh?"

says one of the men. He holds out what looks to me
like a comic book. *The Watchtower*. My mother recoils.
"May we come inside?" says one of the women.
My mother keeps hold of the door. "I'm sorry," she says.

And then, like the girl she was in Sunday School,
rattling off her memory verse: "*For by grace are ye saved
through faith: and that not of yourselves: it is the gift of God:
Not of works, lest any man should boast.*" Her face has gone

a little red. "Ephesians 2:8-9," she adds apologetically.
And she quietly shuts the door in their faces. She turns
to me then—me, watching from the piano bench. She is
trembling. And I know that, somehow, I have been saved.

TWELVE

When I was twelve, I snarled
my uncle's fishing line inside his reel
so badly that he had to cut it with a knife—
not just snip it cleanly off
but slice the entire mess apart.
This was on the meadow lip of Graveyard Lakes,
a day's hike into the Silver Divide.

There were other indignities as well.
The mosquitoes that feasted on my rear
when I dropped my drawers to do my duty.
The mule that out of nowhere sprouted
the biggest erection I'd ever seen.
The other two boys who couldn't stop laughing
whenever I ran to my uncle and cried,
"Uncle Earl! Uncle Earl!"

One evening, the other men asked me
to fill up a cook pot in the spring.
I found a little creek by camp and climbed
and climbed, but could not find
where it came bubbling out of the ground.
So an hour later I came back with an empty pot.
"I couldn't find the spring," I said.
And then I learned they had only meant
the creek itself. And the two boys
laughed and laughed at me.
Uncle Earl! they sang together. *Uncle Earl!*

But that is what it means to be twelve
and scared and clumsy and misinformed,
with an uncle who wants to have your back
but doesn't know how because twelve
is twelve and doesn't get better for a while,
for a very long time, in fact. I just wanted
to be in my bedroom where I could read
about King Arthur and his knights, who
rode into the dark forest and always found
clear bubbling springs and silver fountains
right where they were supposed to be,
coming fresh out of the ground.

ZIAD

His name was Ziad, the only Arab boy or girl
in the eighth grade—in the whole school,
for that matter. What he was doing in Oregon
we didn't know, his father a graduate student, maybe.
I'd like to think I was friendly to him,
shared some of my chocolate milk,
because he was skinny, and scared.

We had a new all-weather track,
there in the fields of the Willamette,
and it looped its endless quarter mile
among honking geese that crossed the clouds
and the liquid song of red-winged blackbirds
in the reeds. We ran for what felt then like distance—
three full laps, thirteen hundred and twenty yards—
and we practiced with serious intent.
Steve Prefontaine was already famous
and four grades ahead of us, just over
the Coast Range in Coos Bay.

One afternoon, however, laboring into the homestretch,
I saw Ziad curled around the wooden edge
of the long-jump pit in the tall grass, trying to stay
out of sight. Our eyes met, and he looked away,
lips quivering with fear or with shame.
I decided then it was cowardice, and decided then
it was no wonder the Israelis had whipped the Arabs

a few months back—whipped them hard
as my father cheered on his side of the television.
Prejudice has its starting guns, and these
were mine. I ran on by to the finish line
and did not speak with him again.

TO BUILD A FIRE

All I ever wanted to do was build a fire
in the rain. To begin with a pile of sodden ash
and ply it with twigs that I would discover,
dry beneath rotting logs in the forest.

To pile those twigs just so, with space enough
for circling air but just the right proximity
to let tiny flame lead on to flame.

And then to add the little sticks
the size of my almost-freezing fingers,
to stack them in careful, miniature teepees
that gradually glow within. And then the wrist-size
pieces of kindling, catching in a conflagration
even as the rain, the sleet, comes pelting down.

And finally the wet-barked rounds,
big as my thighs, roasting for good and long
in the wind, a roaring blaze
that no blizzard could suffocate, not even
the sudden slough of snow from a bough.

To build a fire on such a day would make me feel
complete as a man, gendered to my full estate.
And I would share it with anyone,
even my enemy in the storm.

WHY I MISS HIGH SCHOOL

My friend John was afraid of snakes.
Me too, of course, but not as much.
So, riding my bike back up the hill
from the tennis courts, when I saw
a garter snake in the gutter,
I coaxed it into an empty can
for tennis balls, snapped on the lid,
and placed the can in my basket.
Then I rode to John's and said,
"Want to see my new tennis balls?"
I handed him the can, and the snake
popped out right in his face
before looping underneath the couch.
John screamed a very high-pitched scream.
Then he hit me. But it was worth it.
I would do it again, I thought.

What I did do, with the help
of another friend, was steal his VW Bug
from where it was parked outside the theater
on John's first date with Sarah Youngberg.
The incomparable Sarah Youngberg.
We popped the clutch and push-started it
to a secret spot by the river,
then left a series of notes for them,
a scavenger hunt to find the car.
John did not think this was funny.

The best, though, was when he moved
into an attic apartment with our friend Rick.
This was right after graduation.
Three of us smuggled a girl who liked him,
Twyla Thetford, into his bed
before he came home from scooping ice cream.
We unscrewed all the light bulbs
and then hid in the bedroom closet.
At midnight, John came stomping
up the stairs, tried the light switch,
shrugged his shoulders, dropped
his drawers, and hopped into bed.
Then he screamed that high-pitched
scream again. "Rick said I could
stay here," Twyla said bewitchingly.
Was there time, even, for the snake
to pop out of the can? We couldn't
help it, we started laughing.
John threw open the closet door
and belted us hard, every one.
That John. He was in need
of a little anger management.

WHEN I GOT BACK

When I got back from the Icefield,
my mother said my laugh was different—
more through the nose. I must have picked
it up from that daring young climber,
Eric Reynolds, who had shown me how
to carry an ice ax and tie into a frozen rope.
Eric Reynolds had led the very first ascent
of the Taku Towers just that spring,
the ones that rose across the five-mile-wide
expanse of the Taku Glacier, the glacier
that I measured with a theodolite
from a spacious, cliffside perch of stone.
One night I saw the blood moon rise
and orange sun set on opposite shores
of that river of ice—and then the stars—
and that was nothing to laugh about.
But my mother had lost the boy she knew,
the most delighted sounds from his mouth
a foreign bray, Pinocchio turned into an ass.
I made it up to her, though, in a moment
by snatching a cookie from the glacier
of our freezer—oatmeal, chocolate chip—
and bringing it to the same wide mouth
she had always known. Three years later,
my brother talked her into baking
a thousand cookies—twenty-one batches—
for an expedition to Denali. They lasted, frozen,
for over a month, but my brother came back
without his fingers or his feet. That year,

the only time I saw her smile was when
we told her that Doug Scott, the British climber
of world renown who had helped us down
from that terrible summit—who had arrived
at the summit himself with little more
than a bag of prunes left in his pack—
that Doug Scott said he had never
tasted better cookies in his life.

CATCHING A RIDE, 1975

When the Colonel from Monterey picked me up
at a gas station in Rock Springs, Wyoming,
he said it was my short sleeves—no tracks to hide.
I had just combined a bowl of grapenuts with powdered
milk at a rusty sink in the men's room, having hitched
a day and a night from Sawtooth Ridge in Yosemite.

I never liked traveling east, away from the Sierra Nevada,
but the Colonel (I have forgotten his name)
made it unexpectedly easy at 59 miles per hour,
just four miles above the limit, taking me all the way
to college in the suburbs of Chicago, where
I only missed the first half hour of my biology class.

He was crossing the country to golf with his fellow survivors
of the Battle of the Bulge, which was all he could talk about—
how every one of his field commanders was shot dead
before his eyes, how he became the one in charge
at just my age. He couldn't believe he was still alive,
driving across the summer snow of cornfields in Iowa.

Colonel, I salute you now, steering against those memories
with a boy so full of his own adventures
he hardly had an ear for yours. But violence
makes us generous to our former selves,
I know that now, and in the shadows of gas stations,
of classrooms, I am the one still looking for the ones we were.

II.

Now

PROFESSIONAL DEVELOPMENT

for Jack Leax

My first year of college teaching,
a visiting assistant professor.
And my own office—or half of one—
in a stately red-brick edifice
with a white wooden cupola,
looking out on the autumn hills.

And I, at my desk, lavishing
a freshman essay with comment
after helpful comment, like
so many leaves coming to rest
upon the margins of each thought.

That is when my mentor, the poet,
looked over my shoulder and said,
"Son, you're putting chrome
wheels on a manure spreader."

THIS BLONDE WOOD CHAIR

This blonde wood chair with three
curved slats across the back still shines
a little in the light of afternoon.

Underneath are three more slats
to store your books on while you sit
at the dark table, attentive, or not,
to what your classmates have to say.

They too are sitting in chairs like yours,
which gives you hope of some equivalence
with the others, though you may be intimidated
by their comments on the uses of enjambment
in Shakespeare's Sonnet 29—or 129, was it?

Even your teacher, egalitarian at heart,
squirms in a wood chair just like yours,
straining to listen, straining to say
just what it is that you can hear.

FINAL EXAM

with a prayer from Cymbeline

Under an awning in a parking lot,
I proctor an exam in time of Covid.
It is a week till Christmas, and the sun
beats underneath the tent from its low place
above the islands in the gaping sea.
Each at a desk, the students bend with masks
and pen their thoughts on those who took their lives
in Shakespeare's tragedies—how Romeo
left not a drop of poison on his lips
for Juliet to taste. How Goneril
destroyed herself for spite. How Gloucester too
tried leaping from the brink, so overcome
with sorrow, and Othello with his shame.
Even the ocean spread so bright below
could be where Roderigo yet might choose,
like pigs of old down cliffs of Gadara,
to dive and drown himself incontinently.
The students finish writing, one by one,
and rise in quiet triumph to present
their meditations, thanking me in turn.
And then they take their unregarded leave.
I'm left to pray each one might find their way
into the darkness, through the solstice shade.
And for myself I add this prayer as well:
To your protection I commend me, gods,
From fairies and the tempters of the night.

PLEIN AIR

What is it about an open-sided canopy
that seems both airy and complete?
This one is broad and white on top

with inner billows of purple fabric
asterisked by darkened stars.
We feel a little like royalty here,

the setting sun making us all luminous
as we trade poems and noble comments.
Breezes blow through long-needled pines

beside us, and mourning doves
coo their refrain. We sail together
like Antony and Cleopatra in silken barges

on the Nile, like Aladdin on his carpet,
and who knows when or where
we will land? As Robin Hood lay

dying in an upstairs chamber,
he shot an arrow out the window
that has yet to come to earth.

THIS TIME, THIS PLACE

I'm up on stage, though there is no crowd
below in the auditorium. Just a few
poetry students up here with me, spaced
and seated in an odd assortment of chairs.

One has a wooden arm broken off,
as if it has been thrown across the stage
by an actor in a fit of mock-rage.

Around us the walls are painted black,
but at least the auditorium windows
that look onto the formal gardens
are clear of their shades. Even with

my glasses off (my steaming mask still on),
I can see the orange flare of the birds of paradise
along the straightened walks and hedges.

And nearer at hand, in a corner
of the closest window, a single
sparrow, all in a flutter, keeps on
brushing the glass, trying to get in.

AN ELEGANT LIGHT

When I got to my office this morning,
a crew was thinning a live oak
that had grown into the wooden eaves.

Our building is nearly a century old,
the tree at least that; they are friends.
But some friendships end in fire,
so we prune them back.

The tree now lets an elegant light
into my window. The sinuous trunk
remembers its branches, and so do I.

Both of us, like bodiless souls
newly arrived in clouds of glory,
are trying to decide
how much we miss them.

THE LISTENER

for Kurt Goerwitz

As he sat listening to me in his usual chair,
the sun crept beneath the clouds and through
the window behind him and pierced his ears.
Suddenly, they were red, and glowing,
the flesh and blood alive with light—
like something out of one of those movies
he often tells me I should watch but never do.
But better than that. Something elfish, fairy-like,
as if he were revealed to me, after all these years,
as a being from another realm. To be honest,
I had never really noticed his ears until just then.
But here they were, marked out as the spirited
portion of his presence. These were the wings
on which he could fly his way into retirement,
made strong and tireless and aglow
from all those days of beatified patience,
ready now to attend and ascend.

THINKING OF THE NORTH CASCADES

Out my ancient windowpanes,
tractors grind across the ground—
a new road into campus.
The glass shudders, the floor
shakes, the desk begins to vibrate

like a double bed in a cheap motel,
after you put in the quarter.
Better a thousand boots
than one bulldozer, someone said.
(He was thinking of the North Cascades.)

I used to hear the hammer-song
of acorn woodpeckers, the distant
pok of tennis balls across the lawn.
Now I will hear the revolution
of many tires, the backfiring

of V-8 engines, the slag of DJs,
the incoherent rumbling of bass.
When did we stop putting one thought
after another, slow as speech,
stately as an evening walk?

DETERMINING THE RELATIONSHIP

There's a wooden bench by a pond
where I like to eat my lunch alone.
That pond is left from a private estate
of nearly a century ago.
The oaks and rushes screen it now
from other walks about the college,
a fountain feeds it from within,
and an alabaster figure of
the daughter of Pharaoh, disrobing to bathe,
hesitates upon the shore.

After dark the pond becomes
a place for earnest conversation,
and once I found, half-buried at
my feet, a bra. While eating there
I like to read a poem or two
and sometimes gently fall asleep—
such is my age. One time, however,
I woke to find a tiny note
enfolded in a hidden crevice
of that bench. I opened it.

Dear one, it said. *How many times
I've thought of you, and thought of us—
the pair we'd make—as fitted as
twin birds of paradise in bloom.
The moon is not more anxious to
reflect the sun as I to stand
before your face. And yet—and yet—*

there is a something tells me that
we are not meant for one another's
arms forever. You have your plans,
I mine. Know that I wish you blessing
on your every path, that I
will look back fondly on this very
place, and never will forget
the loving ways you looked at me.
Your lips and hands will always meet
with mine within my memory,
but we must part, as surely as
the seeds of splendid flowers take
their separate ways upon the wind.
Yours ever and yours only, but not yours.

The note filled me with wistfulness
but also with some admiration.
I thought of all those girls from school—
the ones I'd liked but had not liked
me in return—for none had been
this eloquent. And so I printed
at the bottom, in red ink meant
for Valentine's: *Fine metaphors,*
a rich consistency of tone.
Expert ambiguity,
an unambiguous A+.

SUBJECT TO DUST

So says the diamond warning sign
in the broad valley beneath the barren Temblor Range.
And sin, George Herbert would add.

Inside the car, my wife is giving me the business
for sticking to the speed limit of 55 miles per hour,
a parade of pickups on our bumper.

In the back seat, a box full of her mother's ashes.
Later, when it is her turn to drive, I'll resist
when she asks me to read aloud and then reply

to every text that pings her phone.
Toward evening, she insists I call our B&B
to tell them we'll be an hour late

because of Sacramento traffic. "Here,"
she says, "this is the number," pointing to
the screen while keeping one eye on the road.

So, I dial and dutifully say, "We'll soon be late.
I mean, we'll be there later than we hoped,
but soon enough. Please save our spot."

There is a pause.
And a very gracious woman tells me
I have called the mortuary.

UP AND ABOUT

Though lost in a coma since Thanksgiving
    and not at all likely to wake by New Year's,
or Groundhog Day for that matter, let alone
    Easter morning, last night she was up
and about in my dreams—a bit cautious,
    perhaps, but wry and alert as a cricket bat
and ready to get on with things where
    they had been left off. Those research papers
that had to be graded by Christmas, for example.

    "Sorry," I said. "I already marked them."
"Were they any good?" she said.
    "Some better than others."
"Better," she sang, "because they are better!"
    "Like you?" I asked. She brushed that away.
"All that is left," she said, "is to make
    a few poems a little bit worse
than they might have been."
    "Still worth it," I said. But I woke
before she could agree.

THY NECESSITY

Our friend Greg was two weeks shy
of his lingering end when he called to say
he was so sorry we had lost our golden retriever.
You see, he had lost a retriever himself
and knew the private pain of it.
Then there was John, my former colleague,
who, when given his own death sentence,
found a way to console the young oncologist,
telling her what a good job she had done,
and how he was sure it must have been hard
to share the news. How to account
for such men, such moments? Deflection?
Denial? That, of course, but something
deeper and truer as well. Sir Philip Sidney,
mortally wounded in the thigh at Zutphen,
handed his canteen of water to the soldier
sprawled beside him in the field
and said, for pity of his groans,
"Thy necessity is yet greater than mine."

MY MOTHER-IN-LAW'S THIRD HUSBAND
SPEAKS ON REQUEST

You want to know about Hemingway? He was
my neighbor out of Ketchum. Not next-door,
but close. I used to take him hunting in winter,
for mountain lion. Pappy—which is what I called him—
he'd sit in the snow tractor, with Gary Cooper
sometimes, and drink his wine from Nice, France—
the wine he kept in a bota bag. I never did learn
to drink from a bag. Went all over me, just like that.
And he would laugh—my shirt all covered
with that damn stuff. He'd sit there while I took the dogs
and treed a lion. Then I'd hike back through the snow
and bring him out to a regular ruckus, all them pups,
where he'd shoot the thing, and it would drop
clean to the ground. Pappy, he was big and tall.
He called me Shorty. He'd lift me up
and plunk me down right onto the bar stool.
And he was strong. Once, that tractor
ran into some barbed wire and got itself all shit-fouled up.
He got out and cleared that wire against his chest
as if it was nothing. One day, he called and said
he'd just got back from Africa and had a lion skin for me.
That I should come on over and get it. I have to bring
my hay in first, is what I told him. So I brought
the rest of my hay into the barn that morning,
and when I got back to the kitchen, the radio said
that Hemingway had shot himself. Just like that.
I never did go over there and talk with Mary.
Never did get that lion skin.

WHAT THE WIND BLEW
INTO THE CANYON

A photograph of a pair of black Labradors
standing guard over a child.
Palm fronds past the point of praise.
Thick peels of bark from a streamside grove

of eucalyptus. And eucalyptus buttons, blue.
Start times for a district track meet.
A memo to the physical plant, requesting signs
(not wonders) for the campus spiritual institute.

Shriveled olives among the knees of olive trees.
Broken limbs of coast live oak.
Class notes (sociology). A grocery list
(half-and-half). A receipt for gas (premium).

Vacant bags of tortilla chips, of sunflower seeds,
of fertilizer. Clif Bar wrappers. Water bottles.
A Starbucks coffee cup, with cap. A single strand
of barbed wire that disappears into the ground.

NO COMPETITION

The high-strung net behind home plate
is softened by some wisps of lichen.
Year by year the tufts grow deeper,

filamenting, elfin beards that strand
our view. Eventually, all we'll see
is the double play of algae and fungi,

a gray-green wall that separates
us from the field but joins us
to the long surprises of this world.

AT THE BEAUTIFUL GATE

And he took him by the right hand and raised him up. Acts 3:7

How many times have you seen this
on the football field? The hulking tackle,
after the play, reaching down

to the halfback and pulling him up
with a sure, strong grip. Every once
in a while, a player from the other team

will do this for his flattened opponent.
A re-enactment of miracle, of resurrection.
Again and again. Not carted off the turf

this time, but rising with a little help
to stand once more on his own two feet.
What else could you want, really?

Something almost worth the shock
of that hard embrace, of overthrow,
that crash and crush into the earth.

A PORTRAIT OF OUR PATRONESS, OVER THE LIBRARY FIREPLACE

The tight-lipped lean of Mrs. Kerr,
deceased above the Chinese vases.
Their fine blue shine, the rufous
apples and yellowing leaves strung
carelessly across the marble mantlepiece.

The arch of her brow, eyes sharp
and narrow. The way the azure
of her dress joins onto the shapeless
dark, and the way the oils scallop
in the dusky air behind her coif,

held within the gilded frame.
Too, the marks of the adze
on hand-hewn walnut paneling,
the cranberry crush of the carpet,
the empty lectern standing square

before the hollow of the hearth,
the andirons, the marbled gods and
goddesses, bare-breasted goddesses
in flight, their arms raised in relief
into a small and endless marble sky.

CHRIST AND THE ADULTERESS

after Titian

The young man in the foreground,
crouching in impatience as if wanting
more than anything the keys to the car,
is flabbergasted with disbelief,
flaunting his scarlet codpiece as if
he were the one who did the deed.

The buxom whore, her broad skirt
as white and pillowed as sheep
in pasture ready for slaughter,
is leaning without comfort on his left arm.
She's been caught in the act:
this is no time to draw in the dust.

But Jesus grips his other arm,
his right arm, as if to dissuade.
The hold he has on the young man's bicep
is hard to describe—powerful, yes,
but a force, like the stars in the Renaissance,
that does not so much compel as impel.

And the face, lost in a soft focus,
harder to see than any other in that frenzy.
And yet, more there, more definite
in its depth of intention, as if giving approval
to something within the young man
that youth itself does not yet know.

And then, cut out of the picture,
the head of the more middle-aged fellow,
the one in the rose satin cap, turned
just now to wager the outcome,
gazing shrewdly over his shoulder
as if one look could cast a stone.

AARON RECALLS HIS GLORY DAYS

That brother of mine never was much of a climber.
Strong enough—we joked about his golden calves.
But scared of heights, that's for sure. And blind
as a bush at finding the way. Anyhow, it had been weeks—
he hadn't come down. Time to call search and rescue.

In the meantime, though, people started coming to me
with ideas. And I liked being the one they came to.
A slender girl of Ephraim left a set of bracelets
she had stolen from an Egyptian princess.
"You know what to do with these," she said.

Shining goblets showed up at the door of my tent.
Rings for the nose, necklaces, an exquisite figurine
of a cow. It wasn't hard to find the right
metalworkers, the artisans. And the party started
before the image was complete. That lithe and willowy
Ephraimite who slipped me the Egyptian bracelets—
we had a molten time of it, I can assure you.

Until Moses showed up. Stone cold.
Funny how you can resent someone for being saved.

LOQUAT

(Eriobotrya japonica)

The dark green leaves outside
the sashes of my class

are just over a foot long
and half as wide—

more than enough to hide
the shame of our first parents,

and big enough, even, to serve
as diapers for Cain and Abel.

But what I would like to use
them for is leaves on a tree,

where they can rustle quietly
while I run around the lawn

naked, glad to be through
with teaching for another day.

WHAT REMAINS

By late afternoon, he is like a nub of chalk
resting in the dusty tray beneath the board,
like a tattered screen curled up
in its cylinder at the top of its chain.

He turns out the lights and watches
the classroom fade into its learnéd dusk,
then shuffles down the corridor
like a limping conductor taking tickets

he no longer cares to inspect. He is
on his way to the dining car, where
she is already waiting for him,
her elbows denting the tablecloth

as she raises the cut globe of her glass
and gently swirls what remains,
only a single drop of wine
marring the linen of her sleeve.

III.

Near

TRUE WILDERNESS

Today, as I walked, for some strange reason
   I stayed on the road instead of taking the path
      when it came. Am I getting so old

that the asphalt is now a comfort?
   But what if I trust it like a trail,
      look around at the red eucalyptus,

the stream pooling and purling below?
   Each car that passes holds at least
      one questing soul. And the bicycle riders,

the way they lean into the curves
   as their tires spin with such precision—
      even these are part of natural history.

So I let my feet ponder the pavement.
   I take my time, deep in the wilderness
      of this world.

AFTER THE RAIN

When sourgrass bends sweet and heavy
over the path and even the sumac fawns at my feet,
when little streams run large and muddy

under the light of poison oak,
and when tongues of bark hang sodden
from the paling sheen of eucalyptus—

then, then is there moisture enough in my throat
for praise, if only the tiny frogs would return
to bass the bottom of our song.

PRIBET

The nursery at the foot of the hill
does not sell privet—it sells *pribet*.
As if the hedge were a croaking frog

in a bend of the ribber. Eberything
I know suggests they hab got it wrong,
but I pay cash for my fibe-gallon bucket

of pribet, dribe home, dig a bery deep
dibot in the earth, plant it firmly,
and lib happily eber after. The end.

CALIFORNIA WOOD FERN

(*Dryopteris arguta*)

They think I'm friendly,
    the way I wave at everyone.

But it's just a matter of loose
    fronds, a feeling of being

unhinged, a constant fiddling
    with the rachis of my neck.

A little substance would be nice—
    some backbone, some wooden fiber.

Then I would say *Howd'y'do*
    as many times as you please—

not with these flimsy, flailing arms,
    but with a slight nod of the head,

a dip of the crown, lichen
    swaying from my beard.

LATTICE STINKHORN

(Clathrus ruber)

At first I thought you a piece of orange
construction fence, trapped in the ground.
But you were too shapely for that,
appearing and then disappearing into the litter
of oak leaves. Then there was the smell,
the stench of slime within your bulbous cage—
that spore-bearing slime, your gleba—
wafting the scent of rotting meat,
poison to the human tongue but nectar
to the flies who come to celebrate and spread
your seed. In America, you are described
as a wiffleball, as an alien from outer space.
In Yugoslavia, witch's heart.
There, your ovules, before they burst,
are pickled and eaten: devil's eggs.
Do I wish to dine in Yugoslavia? I do not.
But you have arrived on your own terms,
and I welcome you, bubbling
your infested baskets under the trees.

WESTERN WALLFLOWER

(*Erysimum capitatum*)

Wallflower, if I knew how,
    I'd ask you to dance.
But here comes the breeze,
    and you do, all on your own,
orange and trembling.

—*Los Padres National Forest*

OAK CAMP

The live oak shelters a fire ring,
a rusty grill. There is a bleached
log to sit on, worn smooth.
Out of the shade, manzanita tangles
the breeze. And down in a gulley
of shattered stone, a thin stream
apologizes, fading already in May.
Two thousand feet up the mountainside,
it comes from a spring under a boulder
big as a house. You could live in either place—
here by the tree or there by the house—
but you'd have to pick your seasons right.
The snow is deep up high in winter,
and, down here, summer will see
the stream run dry. So you'd probably
go back and forth, the way we do.
The way we almost always do.

—*Los Padres National Forest*

MCKINLEY SPRINGS

One for the people, one for the horses,
both for the bears, and all for the oaks,
the bigleaf maples. The water makes

a quiet talk in the deep ravine,
just the words I wanted to hear
on a dry trail, and just the words

I hear in the night for the moonless hours.
So much to say, and said so well
in that ancient Esperanto of tongues:

You who are thirsty. You. Come.

—*Los Padres National Forest*

A TINY CREEK

Down the bend of this dry ridge,
the sound of water in a crease.
And pooling beneath a sugar pine,
among beds of wild strawberry,
a tiny creek declares itself.

I touch the bark of that fine tree,
immeasurably straight and tall,
and think of sap drawn upward
like a miracle to glistening
cones against the sky.

And I think of juices rising
into red, ripe berries,
not even an inch from the ground.
Once you get going,
no telling where you'll end up.

—*San Rafael Wilderness*

MISSION PINE RIDGE (II)

(*Pinus lambertiana*)

Sun in the top of a sugar pine,
first taste of a May morning.
Limbs reach out as if to touch

the blueing sky on every hand,
offering their green curved cones
perfused with sap as if with honey.

David Douglas quested the length
of the Willamette and then some,
into the drainage of the Umpqua,

to find this fabled tree and its fruit.
To get there he dodged Indians
and grizzly bears, or so he said,

and swam the forks of many rivers.
A few years later, staying as a guest
of friars at Mission Santa Barbara,

did he know these trees were waiting
just a few miles from the sea, their cones
still glistening, still depending?

—*San Rafael Wilderness*

RATTLESNAKES I HAVE KNOWN

None, personally. Just a few of brief
acquaintance. There was the one on a steep,
rocky stretch of trail to Santa Cruz Camp,
sunning itself in thick, fat folds.
It rattled when my friend stepped past it,
unawares, so I stopped short.
We threw gravel, hoping that the snake
would move. But it coiled and rattled
all the more. At last I climbed
below the trail, hearing a sharp
buzz in the sky, fearing it would pour
itself over the edge, into my eye.

Then there was the one over the next ridge,
on Coche Creek. I didn't see it, just heard it
under the poison oak as I passed.
I spent the next five minutes watching
every single step I took, then said to myself,
You ought to look up once in a while,
in case there is something like a bear.
And as soon as I looked up the trail,
a bear flew out of the brush
and landed on all fours on the path.
Then it began to lumber my way.
Our eyes met. And the bear did
an about-face and sprinted off.
I laughed and laughed, I could not stop.
My seventh day, all alone—
it was that funny, apparently.

The one I most remember, though,
was just a mile, if that, above
the San Ysidro Ranch. I had climbed
a path to a stone bench—the McMenemy Bench—
and sat there for a good long hour, immersed
in the sonnets of Shakespeare.
When I finally looked up from my book,
thinking it might be time for supper,
a slender rattlesnake had glided
up out of the chaparral, head raised
below my feet. It was looking right at me,
stone still except for its flickering tongue.
Who might this be? it seemed to ask.
And I was very still as well.
Shall I compare thee to a summer's day?
I thought. *Thou art more lovely and
more temperate. More temperate,*
I emphasized, hoping that the snake
might wish to live up to the compliment.
Then very slowly, I lifted my feet
and climbed over the back of the bench.
And fled. Light-footed, I fled.

I am afraid of snakes. I admit it.
Under laughter there is fear.
But they make me feel alive, too,
in a snaky way I don't quite understand.
That last one crawled out of the manzanita,
as I recall. *Manzanita* means "little apple."
I guess they are still offering what we still want.

—*Los Padres National Forest*

NAMES OF THE CHUMASH

Just when you think the Indians
of the central coast of California
have disappeared out to sea,
their names keep washing up
on the beaches, dunes, and promontories:
Pismo, Nipomo, Jalama.
Hueneme, Mugu, Malibu.
The peaks stand up and word themselves:
Chismahoo, Cachuma, Topatopa.
And the creeks and rivers and waterfalls
keep flowing in their native tongue:
Cuyama, Sisquoc, Nojoqui.
Piru, Sespe, Matilija.
Even our towns speak ancestry:
Lompoc, Ojai, Saticoy.
And the avenues of our cities, they say:
Jonata, "tall oaks,"
Anapamu, "rising place,"
Anacapa, "island mirage."
And don't forget our toxic
landfill, sweet forlorn *Casmalia.*
Even when we try to bury the earth
with garbage, we cannot bury the names.
They haunt us still. They bless us.
They keep us. They keep us,
always, from forgetting,
even when we have forgotten.

THE LONE WOMAN
OF SAN NICOLAS ISLAND

I looked, and lo, there was no one at all. Jeremiah 4:25

My whale-rib shelter on the ridge
is where I sit after supper,
ready to sleep my way to my people.
I went looking for my child,
but she was gone. With everyone.
The sea otters rest on their backs
in the water, but I must float
on this bare ground.
There was a goddess
who built a rainbow
from an island to the shore.
The people could cross,
but not look down. Some did,
and fell into the sea.
They became dolphins,
the first blue dolphins. I see one
now against the sun, weaving
the waves, a lost cousin.
I would ride the back of that dolphin
to my people, to my child.
But I am a bleached whale bone.
I hear voices in the wind.
They are echoes,
I am an echo, sounding,
but no longer here.

GRAVESIDE SERVICE

(*Corvus brachyrhynchos*)

A dead crow with uplifted wing
lay twisted in the street today.

I scooped it with a shovel,
and another crow, this one alive,
then called and called from a neighbor's oak.

As I walked with my burden
to the ravine, the live crow sailed
above my head and landed
in a eucalyptus, calling, calling.

I flung the body in an arc—
its last, short flight—
and turned away, still listening
to the keening one who stayed
and said what little we still have to say.

LOOKING AT US

(Ardea herodias)

There is a great blue heron, we said.
In the backyard. Just standing there.
Looking at us. And it was, in its tallness,
standing there. Looking at us.
The nearest water a goldfish pond,
almost half a mile away. But here
it was, on an August morning.
Patient, wings folded, its implacable eye
atop its impossible neck. We found
the binoculars, crept out onto the porch.
We approached—too far—and the heron
loosed its broad gray wings and climbed
the air and was gone, over a sycamore tree.
There was a great blue heron, we said.
And we looked at each other as if we were,
each one of us, some kind of wonder.

AEOLUS

Morning wind in the live oak trees,
   moving them in bosomy ways,
      one part pulsing, then another.

The breeze blows in
   from Cold Spring Saddle,
      thence from north of Point Conception,

the open sea, gathering freshness
   from whales, olives, ceanothus,
      billowing the breasted branches,

scattering the hooked green acorns,
   planting them with warm, full breaths,
      with little sighs.

UNDER LIVE OAKS

(Quercus agrifolia)

Smooth little acorn—curved
like a claw, like a twisted
teardrop—autumn rain is planting

you like hopscotch beneath its feet.
Some years, more of you;
other years, hardly any.

But this year, a mast year,
I mash you into the street,
the sidewalk, with my heel.

Little boys collect you in buckets
and fling you hard at one another.
And overhead, among the white

bones of the branches of eucalyptus,
acorn woodpeckers prepare
a private place for you—

a pocket, a nest, perfectly fitted—
where you will wait, where you will
perch, forgotten in the winter fog.

COTTONWOODS

(*Populus fremontii*)

This hidden grove of cottonwoods
    in a high ravine, as close to the ocean
        as they dare, is where I climb
            around my birthday each November.

Even in drought, a little creek
    pools in the shade, and most years
        the leaves are yellow,
            illuminated by mid-day sun

in a sky that is almost always blue.
    Dark-green laurel make a fragrant
        understory, and the wind
            comes and goes as it will.

I sit on the same round sandstone
    boulder by the path and think about
        the months gone by, then wonder
            when I will retire from waving

my brittle limbs in a classroom.
    The trees aren't telling. They just say
        it is autumn again, the way it could be
            for anyone without his even knowing it.

—*Los Padres National Forest*

AFTER VANCOUVER

Around the sun that shines within the trees,
the fog disseminates whatever light
pervades the morning on the pastured hill.
Our trail cuts through poison oak, then sage,
the vegetative indecisiveness
of California's undulating coast.
Just south of here, in 1793,
Vancouver saw the shore in flames for miles
from the darkened decks of *The Discovery*,
the air afoul with ash, *vast volumes of*
this noxious matter blown far out to sea.
He thought that he had sailed his ship to hell,
but it was just a sight along the way
to home in London, infamy in the press,
a caning on the street, and painful death
from natural causes at the age of 40.
Two centuries and more beyond his time,
we hike this path in cloud, our prospects dimmed,
the hills more prone than ever to combust.
But still, the smell of sage, the perfect shine
of poison oak among live oaks and shade—
our place, our moment, where we may receive
the light of fire, of fear, of healing wings.

A PERFECT FURNACE

A thick bank of fog across the beach
this morning—except it is not fog
but smoke, tinged by the dawn
into something almost beautiful.

During the night, a fire in the chaparral
bloomed like a star in the east,
we none the wiser save for our flickering
lamps, our noble fir bright-lit, then not.

The air above the mountains here
is blue and pure in December cold.
But a day's walk down *El Camino Real*,
a perfect furnace of suffering.

THE FIRE-BALD MOUNTAINSIDES

The fire-bald mountainsides—
    and came the rain, and then
        the scouring mud, the boulders,

doing glacier's work in minutes.
    Confusing and confounding
        roads and houses. Lives.

I cannot tell you all,
    but when it stopped
        there were by later count

one thousand pets in search
    of homes, in search
        of outstretched hands.

ABOVE TANGERINE FALLS

(*Populus fremontii*)

The little grove of cottonwoods in the fold
    behind the sandstone brink—that little grove

is gone today, but head-high shoots
    with little leaves mark where it stood.

The creek bed forms, reforms, and whirls
    apart at will, and limbs and tendrils

surf the waves of shifting soil.
    The mudslide just three years ago

meant death for some beneath the canyon.
    Here, it merely rearranged the life to come.

—*Los Padres National Forest*

HOLLOW AGAIN

(*Quercus agrifolia*)

Look at this trunk, burnt hollow,
   keyholed from side to side.
      Yet, in spite of a few dead limbs,
         a crown of leaves pushes against

the patient sky. So we might
   flourish, in spite of ourselves,
      evacuated of fortitude. Paul
         said it: in weakness, strength;

in death, life. I don't know how.
   But most days, a long resilience
      of xylem and phloem.
         Of chlorophyll. *Ex nihilo.*

THE VIRGIN AND THE MUSEUM
OF NATURAL HISTORY

Out the back of the museum, across the footbridge,
through the native Chumash garden, among the quiet
of live oaks, along the path and up the steps,
and just beyond the sign that says,
No Trespassing: Violators Will Be Prosecuted,
there is a forgotten veranda, covered with leaves
of pittosporum, just beneath an equally forgotten grotto.
And in that grotto, standing on a pedestal
of mortared stone from the creek below,
stands the patient Virgin Mary, robed in white
and hands uplifted, pressed together palm to palm.
Her eyes are closed in adoration,
but you get the feeling she is quite aware
of your presence—you, now, seated on a dusty
ledge among clouds of ivy and wilded roses
at her feet. If someone is going to prosecute you,
she will not be the one to do it. And the Virgin Mary,
through her closed eyes, seems to see not only
your bewildered self, weary and wanting,
but everyone and everything in the canyon below—
the swallowtails in their pavilion,
the tyrannosaurus rex named Sue,
the rambling, silent grizzly bear
in the evening gloom of his display.
She sees each artificial star within the planetarium,
and the man who announces the daily show
on a hidden microphone in the dark.
Through her closed lids the Virgin sees

the woman arranging books in the gift shop,
the children leaping from rock to rock,
the keeper holding a kestrel falcon on its perch
with wounded wing. The Virgin Mary
blesses them all, every one, from her hidden
grotto of ivy and roses, and they do not even know
she is there. And as you rise and as you leave
to place your feet once more secure
on legal grounds, you carry this secret deep
within you, this secret of a mother who watches
through closed eyes, who guards your steps,
who knows your presence on this earth.

IV.

Far

FALLING

You feel the falling forward first
as eminence, the domain of the world
all before you. Then you realize
the terrain is now too steep for safe
descent, the scree too loose,
the boulders too precarious. Dislodged,
they tumble with your steps—
no longer steps but bounding flight
above a slope long past the angle
of repose. The gravity of your situation
begins to mount. But before you
land in a distant field of debris,
before flesh is torn and blood erupts,
you feel and know the glory of it,
the mastery of earth beneath you—
you, for the moment,
a prince of the power of the air.

FRANKLIN LAKES

Said the gibbous moon
to the foxtail pine,
Just hold me for a while.

—*Sequoia National Park*

EARTH HAS NOT ANY THING TO SHOW MORE FAIR

For my money, emphatically not the city of London
from Westminster Bridge. Though, admittedly,
Wordsworth did find himself in a raw moment
there in the dawn on the top of that coach
en route to France to see his old flame,
Annette Vallon, and their nine-year-old daughter,
Caroline, to ask permission to marry,
at last, a woman from the Lake District.

My own turn on that bridge was late afternoon,
the height of traffic, the old city a noisy glare.
That's why I would nominate this pond-sized meadow,
spring green, ringed with the sun-warmed,
dusky trunks of sequoia trees, glowing here
in the quiet as they have these thousand years
and more. There is no bridge except for the log
I am sitting on beside the trail, telling myself
I can walk yet farther but knowing I must turn
around to recover my camp by sunset,
and my wife still waiting for me beyond.

An evening wind sounds now in the dark
green luster of branches—so far over my head
they might as well be in another country—
a true country. And the one crow that is cawing
there is calling from another time.

—*Sequoia National Park*

HERD OF SHEEP IN THE FOREST
OF FONTAINEBLEAU

after Charles-Emile Jacque

So, I like those big trees—old growth,
we would call them. And the sheep right alongside—
perfect, pastoral co-existence. And though
we are in France, in the Forest of Fontainebleau,
around 1870 or so, my mind drifts to the mountains
of the American West at just about that time—
to John Muir following his wooly locusts
up across the branches of Yosemite Creek
to the pastures of Tuolumne. But then came
more sheep, and more, and the meadows sank
into dust and mire, and Muir pressed for a national park,
in large part to keep out the lambs. And the park
came, and the sheep were banned, but still
they were herded into the meadows, where the shepherds
played hide-and-seek with the U.S. Cavalry—
the Buffalo Soldiers, they were called,
because they were black. And then Gifford Pinchot
invented the U.S. Forest Service, and sheep were just
fine with him, and John Muir felt betrayed
and parted ways with Pinchot forever.
All because of some sheep in the woods,
which seem beautifully appropriate in the opinion
of Charles-Emile Jacque. But who knows?
Maybe the French had figured it out over the years
and brought their sheep in smaller numbers.

Last summer, in Piute Meadows, just outside
of Yosemite, the Forest Service allowed a band
of four hundred sheep to graze. They trampled a path
ten miles long and sixty feet wide to reach the grass
of the West Walker, and when they got there,
they parted around us where we stood
as if they were the Red Sea, pouring
in divided streams. The beauty
of that motion was such that we felt alive
to be among them, even as we regretted their presence.
Which is how I feel, sometimes, as a secret
admirer of disaster. The fire that once burned our home
was lovely in its own way, and face it,
there was even something darkly aesthetic
about the bloom of smoke and flame
at the top of the World Trade Center.
Which makes me think once again
of that seemingly deciduous sequoia
in the foreground, the sheep nibbling
about its roots, full of years, and about to fall.

YOSEMITE LOVE POEM

Your breasts are like twin waterwheels
    in the rush of the Tuolumne.

Your knees are like young lodgepole pines
    bent under snow.

Your toes are like smooth pebbles
    at the foot of Bridal Veil Falls.

And your speech is like
    the curve of current at the brink.

But what am I? More like the ashes
    underneath the old, retired firefall.

A squat Pacific chorus frog
    *wreck-ec*king from a granite crack.

The bear who gets his paws immersed
    in pancake batter in the campground.

You, the shapely curve of Half Dome;
    I, that missing half in air.

IT GOES

From our campsite on Return Creek,
we had scrambled up and over the massive
blocks of Grey Butte and down a grassy gulley

to the terraced outlet of Soldier Lake.
Now we lifted up our eyes to a granite shoulder
above the water that rose to join the ridge above.

Just where it met the rim of the cirque,
the shoulder steepened. *Would it go?*
The age-old question that the former climber

in me wanted to answer. If not, we thought,
then lunch back here at the dark-blue lake.
We rounded the heathery verge and flushed

a dignified but slightly ruffled ptarmigan
(its young close by), then up
the polished shoulder till it reared.

And lo, a hidden ledge appeared, square-cut
holds, a ramp inside an open book.
My arms and shoulders filled with a joy

they had not felt for many a month—
certainly not in the last two days as we
stumbled up the trail under heavy packs.

I'm 64, I thought to myself, but my body
remembers what it could do when it was
careless, confident, and just 18. Age comes,

yes, but there is a continuity we call ourselves.
Sometimes it speaks in the touch of hands
and feet upon a rising rock. It comes. It goes.

—*Yosemite National Park*

PARKER PASS LAKE

Was ever a lake so electric blue?
Surely some trick of aquarium lighting,
some displacement of tropical seas.

Not the clouding of glacial flour
but the clear intensity of perception,
the entire surface one un-occluded eye.

Bluest in sun, that is true, but even
as thunderheads gather of an afternoon,
the depths retain a luminescence,
a robust thisness of expression.

We're here, the waters say.
We're here in case you didn't notice
the untold miracle of your life.

—*Yosemite National Park*

BEARPAW MEADOW (II)

First light in the incense cedar,
rush of the Kaweah below in spring flood.
Otherwise, the sloping meadow dim
and silent, a few rounded drifts of snow.

Here on the forest edge, the pyramid
of our rain fly, perfectly pitched
among white fir, and a flat stoop
of granite to sit on while we wake.

Last night I dreamed I couldn't
remember what day of the week it was.
I asked all the people I met,
but they only thought I was kidding.

We would be willing to linger with the deer
and the marmots—the bears, even—
resting on this granite porch
until we have absolutely no idea.

—*Sequoia National Park*

GREAT WESTERN DIVIDE

The first of morning on the mountains
flushes them with shame
to be uncovered from the arms of night.

The forest in the Big Arroyo
sleeps in shadow, unaware.

Between, the granite pearls
into presence, and the banks of snow
keep shining, as they always do,

little ponds in which the stars
can see themselves before they go.

—*Sequoia National Park*

CALIFORNIA, CALIFORNIA

Striding down Shepherd Creek from Anvil Camp
    in early morning, out of the timberline
        foxtail pine across fragrant slopes
           of chinquapin, of manzanita,

we feel the risen sun in our faces
    and see it lighting the feathery styles
        of mountain mahogany all before us,
           leathery leaves on twisted trunks

transformed into bearers of flame.
    Our feet find rhythm on the old,
        improbable trail, raising the dust
           over shifting talus and hardened flows,

and we say in our minds, *California, California.*
    Behind us, at the foot of the pass,
        a herd of deer lies dead and rotting
           in the tail of an avalanche track,

their shanks and fur scattered across the mountainside
    by gravity, wind, and the teeth of coyotes.
        It all depends where you are in the moment,
           whether the landscape gives or takes.

And I do not know how long we will
    be saying this. But the sun
        in the mahogany styles like tongues of fire,
           the roar of the creek now far below us

in the canyon—they have been speaking a long,
   long time, and will still be speaking
      when we lie scattered across the slopes,
         dust beneath other boots and paws.

In other words, the light goes on,
    whether darkness gathers it in or not,
      illuminating what remains,
        California, California.

—*John Muir Wilderness*

TOMAHAWK LAKE

Bilberry bleeds the granite,
   and amber grasses tuft themselves
      for a fallow taste of October sun.

The water hands its jewels
   to the breeze as if the ice
      will never come.

We are the ones, stepping softly,
   resting our heels
      in not quite the same lake,

who bring the ache,
   who sing an elegy
      for the living.

—*John Muir Wilderness*

TECHNICAL CONDO

The barbecue on the balcony
almost exploded at my touch,
though I did get the woodstove
working on the third try.

One look at the directions
for the remotes to the DVD,
the television, the stereo,
and I turned tail.

And the microwave,
with its panel of options,
convinced me to eat my turkey cold.

Even the lockbox on the door,
with its combination and hidden levers,
is enough to keep me standing
outside with the stars.

It is strangely beautiful out here,
no instructions needed
for the light to travel all this way.

—*Mammoth Lakes, California*

SOLAR SYSTEM

Round and round six planets go—
the ones we can see, the one we are on.
Mercury racing, swift of foot,
Venus orbiting behind.
Earth respectful, third in line,
and Mars, taking its martial time.
Jupiter, giant and sedate,
and Saturn, ringed, resting as far
as eye can know. And the sun,
that crackling ball of flame,
the cynosure of all the rest,
all of the planets circling the fire
to get out of the smoke, to find a log
on which to sit in a rustic row,
cooling their heels in the emptiness
of that dark forest, that sable field.

THE RIVER FRIO

Deep in the heart of Texas, we used to sing.
It was about a boy named Texas, and a lost
knife, and where that knife ended up.
We sang it with such glee, too.

But here, now, high above the River Frio,
I never thought it would look
like this, a bleed of green
below the rim of a limestone canyon.

Little clouds scoot west across a plain
horizon of juniper, and hawks and buzzards
sail the thermals, looking to lick
the blood of that poor little boy.

ELEGANT BRODIAEA

(*Brodiaea elegans*)

Brodiaea, I had no idea who you were
until my brother happened to name you
from the saddle. He didn't know
the umbelled flowers with grassy leaves
you grew among, the ones that look like yarrow,
but aren't. And neither did I,
till I looked them up the next morning.
"Yampah," I told him. "Yampah," he said—
"I knew that. A tributary of the Green
in Colorado. Or Utah, maybe."

But your six petals, lavender and
lily-like, will be easy to remember—
and three white stamens rounded
in your delicate throat. My brother
said he knew a lawyer with the first name
of Brodiaea. "Given to him by his parents
or adopted by himself?" That, he said,
he didn't know. This lawyer represents
the wild. As do you, Brodiaea.
As have you ever, brief, in the open.

—*Cascade-Siskiyou National Monument*

YOU, COLORADO

Bending through the open flats
of Havasu, hoping to make it to the Gulf,
you wonder where your current's gone,
why you are shaded by London Bridge.

You were so much better off
beneath the dories of Major Powell,
when you still had an even chance.

Now you are fodder for jet skis,
for cigarette boats, ripple and foam
regurgitated in their smoke, then
slicking into that foreign stillness.

But looking down at you this morning
through a varnished desert slot,
I have the feeling you'll be back,

following your natural course,
your true career, after we have followed
ours to its mechanical collusion.
London Bridge is falling down.

BAKER CREEK

"Maybe we can build a trail down to the creek,"
my brother says. So we part a curtain of ripe
cherries behind the lawn, slip beneath a bigleaf maple,
and follow a fence through sword fern to a drop-off.

I point a way past massive trunks of Douglas fir,
but he favors a gulley of blackberry vines,
head-high. So in we go, submerged in a sea
of light-green thorns until we are swimming
a deer path across a narrow, grassy shelf.

We follow it past a grand fir to a root-webbed
landing by a pool, dark and deep and calm as a doe.
Whether a real trail can follow, we don't know,
but here we are, streamside, a brace of brothers
at the bottom, our boots by the water we have only
seen from above. And that's getting somewhere.

—*McMinnville*, Oregon

ALMOST THERE

Hours after holding my new grandsons
for the first time, I dreamt this:
Out of a chaos of missing persons,
missing papers, I climbed to the top
of Sawtooth Ridge in Yosemite
from Slide Canyon on the south.
Others were with me, ahead and behind,
guides I had worked with in the Sierra.
On the crest of the ridge we one by one
turned toward the westering sun,
not scrambling over blocks and towers
but strolling along a perfect pitch
of polished granite. The going was easy,
the air around us rich and bright and pure and full.
By then we were strung far apart,
and for a moment I had the ridgetop
almost entirely to myself. The friend
I could see in front of me was just starting
to drop down a hidden ramp into deep
shadow, where I would follow,
down where the remnant glaciers rested
on the north. I was wearing a full pack—
we all were—but it had no weight,
my shoulders were steady, I was walking,
walking in the light, the world falling away
before me, just where I wanted to be.

Acknowledgments

Alba: "Western Wallflower"

Askew: "Falling" and "Determining the Relationship"

Banyan Review: "Oak Camp" and "Tomahawk Lake"

Barbizon, Realism, and Impressionism in France (Westmont Ridley-Tree Museum of Art): "Herd of Sheep in the Forest of Fontainebleau"

Cathexis Northwest: "Mission Pine Ridge (II)"

Christian Century: "After the Rain," "At the Beautiful Gate," "Catching a Ride, 1975," "Final Exam," "Hollow Again," and "Thy Necessity"

Cloudbank: "Yosemite Love Poem"

Cold Mountain Review: "Pribet"

The Curator: "The Virgin and the Museum of Natural History" and "What Remains"

Final Exam (Brooks Street Books): "Professional Development"

Forbidden Peak: "Elegant Brodiaea" and "Lattice Stinkhorn"

Hawaii Pacific Review: "Names of the Chumash"

JuxtaProse: "The River Frio"

Leaping Clear: "Great Western Divide," "A Tiny Creek," and "What the Wind Blew into the Canyon"

Miramar: "Cottonwoods" and "Technical Condo"

Moving Forward, Looking Back (Santa Barbara Museum of Natural History): "The Lone Woman of San Nicolas Island," "Rattlesnakes I Have Known," and "Solar System"

Pilgrimage: "Bearpaw Meadow (II)"

Pinyon Review: "Somewhere to Follow" and "You, Colorado"

Poems for Ephesians: "By Grace Are Ye Saved"

Presence: "McKinley Springs"

Rabid Oak: "California, California"

Salt: "After Vancouver" and "Subject to Dust"

Santa Barbara Literary Journal: "To Build a Fire"

Santa Fe Literary Review: "Franklin Lakes"

Sehnsucht: "Looking at Us"

Spillway: "The Fire-Bald Mountainsides"

Triggerfish Critical Review: "Almost There"

Turtle Island Quarterly: "Aeolus" and "Baker Creek"

We Are All God's Poems: "Plein Air"

Weber: "Twelve"

Westmont Campus Biodiversity: "California Wood Fern" and "Graveside Service"

Whale Road Review: "Crime and Punishment" and "In Fear of Art"

Windhover: "Christ and the Adulteress" and "Earth Has Not Any Thing to Show More Fair"

"Names of the Chumash" and "The Virgin and the Museum of Natural History" also appeared in *Moving Forward, Looking Back* (Santa Barbara Museum of Natural History).

This book was set in Centaur, designed by the American typographer and book designer Bruce Rogers, who was commissioned to create an exclusive type for the Metropolitan Museum of Art (New York) in 1914. Based on the Renaissance-period printing of Nicolas Jenson around 1470, it was named Centaur after the title of the first book designed by Rogers using the type: *The Centaur*, by Maurice de Guérin, published in 1915. Lanston Monotype of London cut the commercial version of Centaur and released it in 1929.

This book was designed by Shannon Carter, Ian Creeger, and Gregory Wolfe. It was published in hardcover, paperback, and electronic formats by Wipf and Stock Publishers, Eugene, Oregon.